Dedication

To the Kruse Crew

Thank you for being my people. Losing Dad affected all of us collectively, and yet each of us in different and deep ways. We've stumbled through this grief, and often took it out on each other. Through all of the pain we've had to endure, we still came back to each other, over and over again. I'm so happy I am yours, and forever grateful you are mine.

Mom,
Thank you for being my mom. It's a silly thing because you didn't necessarily know what you were getting when you decided to have a kid, but I'm glad God gave me to you. You teach me how being a good human is being kind and showing up for people. That everyone deserves a little more grace than you are inclined to give. I will forever be in awe of the woman you are.

Ron and Zach,
Thank you for making me tough. For poking fun at me and never letting me get too full of myself. Thank you for being men our dad is proud of. You both remind me of him in the most extraordinary ways. He'll live on with us and through us because of the pieces the three of us carry.

Dad,
Thank you for teaching me what true bravery is. That it is honesty. it's showing your bruises and scars, telling the truth about them, and yet not letting them break you. Thank you for getting

treatment, even if it didn't keep you around as long as we wanted it to. Thank you for being a person that nobody will be able to replace. I love you, and you taught me more in your fifty short years than you will ever get to know.

Preface

This book was supposed to be fifty other things before it became what it is before it ended up in your hands. At first, it was going to be my dad's life story. I was going to be his ghostwriter, and we were going to write his tale of all that he was. While that is still a huge part of this story, he is no longer here to help me tell it. He passed away from Glioblastoma brain cancer on September 9, 2022. We just thought we had more time, and I don't feel right writing that book without him here to correct me (though who knows, maybe I'll get the courage/gaal at some point).

When he started to get really sick, I decided that this would instead be about my gap year. I wanted to write about the sacred year we were going to have as we helped him walk to Eternity. Instead, that walk ended before I even really started writing.

So here I sat, with an ache in my heart to write through my pain and to honor him, without a purpose. I had already picked out this title, and yet I was staring down an empty year. That was until I realized that I had already lived a sacred year. That is the only word that I can come up with to describe the last year that my dad was on Earth; sacred.

This is a collection of short essays that I wrote as I processed life without my dad. It is written in semi-chronological order, beginning when we took my dad home on hospice and on. However, I reference many things that happened during the fourteen months he had cancer, as well as his life before.

While it is deeply personal, the experience of grief is a universal one. I share this with you for many reasons. Because my dad was special, and he deserves to be spoken about. Because grief can feel so incredibly isolating, and I hope that by me sharing my soul you find a friend on your journey. Because my dad loved my writing, and I know that this is a wonderful way for me to honor him.

A couple of things before you begin. My dad decided that his cancer was not a journey, but rather a trek. He wrote about how he had a positive connotation to the word journey, with it being tied to one of his favorite things, traveling. There was "nothing positive or fun about this". So it became his trek, and that is how I will refer to it in this piece of work.

Another important thing to understand is what exactly happened on his trek. He was diagnosed with Stage Four Glioblastoma brain cancer in late July 2021 after having a seizure at home. This is one of the most deadly types of cancer, with an average survival rate of only eight months.

He had three brain surgeries, one experimental treatment plan, and LOTS of chemo and radiation. In the beginning, we believed that he could be a part of the 5% of people who made it past five years with his type of cancer. This was because he was young, active, and because of where his tumor was.

When he had a regrowth in February, we were devastated. It coming back after only seven months meant that his frontline treatment was not working. But, just like after his first surgery, he returned to normal life within a matter of weeks after surgery. One of my favorite videos of him during his time is him with a hospital gown on, doing lunges on the hospital couch. He was an absolute badass, and I hope I can communicate that to you well throughout this book.

Until July 2022 he worked, traveled, and coached. We went to Hawaii, I graduated from undergrad, and we made many wonderful memories together. But, in July he had surgery again for another tumor that had regrown in May. One of my dad's doctors (I honestly forget which one because he had a million), explained to us that Glioblastoma tumors never fully go away. They get as much of them out as they can, but they have "tentacles" that they can not see. Those stay behind and are the reason that this cancer is so deadly.

After a saga of events, we took our dad home to hospice on August 19, and he passed away three weeks later on September 9, 2022. The fact that this part of his life was only fourteen months is mind-numbing to me. It feels seconds and also years long.

Finally, I want you to understand how my dad dealt with his cancer. We knew from the very beginning that this would be the thing to take him, and he accepted it fully. The hardest part of all of this for him was leaving my mom. That was the thing that moved him to tears the most, more than cancer, more than losing his future, it was leaving her behind.

He always hated when people said that he was "fighting" cancer because that would mean that when he died, he lost. And if he was anything, he was competitive and he was a winner. He managed to not fight, yet not give up. He did all the treatments and showed up for all the scans. And yet, he lived his life like he was dying. He reconnected with old friends, took a LOT of trips, and let people know what he thought. He lived his last fourteen months of life like he had lived the 48 years beforehand, on his terms.

May this short piece of work comfort you, push you, and maybe help you feel more understood. I hope that my sharing some of the most vulnerable thoughts I had along this journey helps someone in some way. I'm not one of those people who think we go through hard things to help others, but I do know that hard things can make us more empathetic, compassionate people. I hope sharing this grief journey helps you and me both get there.

Changing

August 25, 2022, Two Weeks Into Dad on Hospice

I hope I'm never the same. I hope my dad and the twenty-two years that he was a part of my life on Earth, I hope they are not something to get over. But in the same breath, I miss being twenty-two. I miss slamming doors and getting in trouble for stupid things and fighting for no reason. I miss the normal where I was the one being taken care of, the one that was about me.

And it's selfish to miss the spotlight. But I don't miss it in a *wanting to be the center of attention* way (okay maybe a little), but mostly in *our normal was a good normal* way. I miss my parents whispering about "adult problems" instead of being intimately involved in them. I miss vaguely knowing my dad's friends, instead of deeply understanding the good and shitty ways that they all grieve. I miss being a kid, being his kid.

I hate that I've changed and I now can not stand to be around some of his people because they just do not grieve well. I hate how mad some of them make me. I hate that I focus on the shitty ones instead of the good ones, especially when the ratio is about 10:1. I hate how heavily I judge people for not knowing how to help the family of a man who is fifty and dying of terminal brain cancer.

They never tell you that when someone dies, they take away their role in your life, too. Craig Kruse died, and so did my dad. It's weird, to be able to mourn those two things and yet also mourn them separately. I'll miss the way that Craig Kruse had a tin of mints in his car that I would always threaten to empty everywhere. I'll miss my dad, and how he made me feel safe to be myself and joke around with him.

Changing due to grieving is strange because it can be good, but you aren't happy that this is the person you are becoming, because the reason is shitty. I like who I am today much more than the girl I was before we found out my dad was sick. I think I am kinder, more empathetic, and more understanding. I'm tougher, wiser, and more mature. I know when to just apologize, and when it is worth the fight. More than anything, I know I do not know a lot, and that I'm lucky that I've got a lifetime to learn.

I just wish my dad could see the woman I've become after he started to decline. I wish that I could show him how I try to not argue with my brothers because I choose to love them over proving that I'm right. That I finally told the guy that I loved him. That I stepped up and helped my mom with all of the selflessnesses that I can muster.

I know that he would be and is proud of me. But I just wish that I could hear him say it, just one more time. But now I'm being greedy because that would not be nearly enough.

I'm scared of how I'll change when he dies. When he isn't here to remind me that everything snowballs, I need to make tiny right choices every single day. I've been consuming a lot of content about grief and loss, and I'm scared that I am going to lose it. That I am going to undo the woman I have become because of my dad's terminal cancer and ruin it when all I have is a dead dad.

I'm afraid that when that is all I have I will run back, chasing the spotlight. That I'll be the kid who can not grieve well, who draws attention to herself by drinking a little too much or not going right back to work and being okay. I'm afraid that this is going to suck the life, and the faith, right out of me. That I'll give my mom even more things to worry about that she just should not have to, especially with navigating being a widow.

I'm afraid I'm going to get drunk and tell some people off. People who inserted themselves, who ran in the other direction, and who just said the wrong thing. Who told my dad to "keep fighting"; the reason he was dying was that he wasn't trying hard enough. I'm afraid I'm going to ruin relationships my dad isn't here to repair because some of his people just suck at being good people in a time of crisis.

I'm afraid I'll become one of those people. I will think because my dad died that I am the grief expert. I'm afraid that sometimes when you change, you can not control and manipulate it. Sometimes you just change, and there is no going back.

Missing Him

September 9, 2022

My dad died today, and it was a relief, for him and us. But I just wish that I could see how he is doing. I want to call him and ask him how heaven is. If he got to meet all the loved ones who have been up there for a while. If he got his strength back and then some. If he is lifting and fishing or if he has found a new hobby.

I used to talk to him almost every day. If it wasn't a phone call, it was a text. A quick "luv u" sprinkled throughout each other's days.

He died a day after the Queen of England. I want to ask him if he got to meet her and if she was fun now that she didn't have to worry about her cheating son or being married to her third cousin.

I want to hug him. To feel tiny in his arms. To feel safe. I want him to be here to protect me from the grief of losing him.

I'm just sad, sad to have lost him, sad to understand the depths of what I have lost, and sad to watch my brothers and my mom go through it, too.

I just miss him.

A Life Well Lived

Craig Kruse's Obituary

Craig Laurence Kruse, 50, passed away peacefully surrounded by his loving family on September 9, 2022. The son of Ron and Roxanna Kruse, he was born in Belleville, Illinois on August 31, 1972. He was raised in Hersher, Illinois where he discovered his passion for athletics. This included him helping secure a runner-up state championship title in football during the 1988-1989 season at Herscher High School and going to State in the shot put his senior year.

He continued his athletic career at Augustana College in Rock Island, Illinois. He was a four-year starter on the football team and placed fifth at Outdoor Nationals in the shot put his senior year. Though none of this compared to his true victory, meeting the love of his life, Kristen, during his freshman year. The two celebrated 26 years of marriage in June and built a wonderful family that Craig was extremely proud of.

Craig also excelled in academics, graduating as an Academic All-American from Augustana, and then obtaining a Master's in Kinesiology from Eastern Illinois University before gaining his Master's in Physical Therapy with highest honors from Emory University. He was a passionate physical therapist for 24 years. Through his work, he positively impacted so many lives by helping others heal and making the recovery process fun along the way.

However, Craig's true passion was coaching. He spent much of his children's youth coaching them and was a huge part of the Hinsdale Falcon's football and wrestling feeder programs. Craig had such an impact on youth sports that the field at Brook Park was recently renamed Craig Kruse Field. This is an honor that is both humbling and also well deserved. Craig pulled the best out of his players, and the coaches around him, because he truly believed in people and their potential.

As his children grew, he became the Strength and Conditioning Coach at Hinsdale Central where he helped athletes from all teams each and every day. Craig eventually began coaching both football and women's throwing at the high school and thoroughly enjoyed being such an integral part of so many athletes' lives. He will be remembered for his care, compassion, and work ethic by the Red Devil community.

His life ended far too soon due to stage four glioblastoma brain cancer. Craig lived for fourteen months after his diagnosis and lived well. He continued to work, coach, and travel for most of the last year of his life. He will be remembered by the phrase he coined "Boots On" because he did not want to "die before he died". He decided to continue to live every day and die with his boots on.

He is survived by his loving wife Kristen, his children Cassie, Ron, and Zach, his parents Ron and Roxanna, his sister Carrie, his nieces Claire, Addie, and his nephew Ian. He has left for them an incredible legacy that they will carry on for him because he taught them how.

Craig is preceded in death by his paternal grandparents; Laverne and Alice Kruse, his maternal grandparents Earl and Yvonne Thompson, and his brother Gregory Paul Kruse, who he now finally has the chance to meet after a lifetime apart.

Eulogy

Delivered at his Funeral on September 15, 2022

Craig Laurence Kruse was a lot of things to a lot of people. A husband, son, brother, uncle, friend, coach, physical therapist, and co-worker. But for three lucky people, he was Dad. He was the one who showed Ron and Zach where to put their fingers on a football for a perfect throw, how to put a boat in the water, and what it means to be a good man. A man who is caring, hard-working, honest, and loving. He showed me how to shoot a free throw, tried to teach me how to throw a shot put, though that one was unsuccessful, and how good life is an honest one.

Our dad valued honesty more than most. When Ron and I were little, he caught us in a lie and this resulted in Ron having to mow an acre of grass and me running two miles. Though one of the more unpleasant experiences of our respective childhoods, this experience left a lasting impact on Ron and I. Ron wrote his college essay about this acre of mowing, and what it taught him about hard work. I became a better liar.

I lied to myself a lot throughout dad's illness like I'm sure most of you would have done and did. First, the lie was that all of our lives were effectively over. That this was the end of our family. And then I became a denier and disguised it as hope that he would be one of the outliers.

Our dad did neither of these things. He decided that if this was how he had to leave this earth, he was going to do it honestly. He never pretended that this impossibly hard trek was easy, or bearable most of the time. and I think that this was my favorite thing about him, and how he left his mark on my life. He was brave because he was honest. The mark he has left on this earth and his people is all the more beautiful and important because he taught the rest of us that we don't need to hide away from pain to continue to live. That our pain will not break us.

That's what boots on really means. Should someone who recently found out they had terminal brain cancer and brain surgery participate in a Strongman competition two weeks later? Probably not. But his boots were on. Should that same person continue to work full-time and work out at 4 am? Probably not, but his boots were on. Should he also throw in the Master's shot put, participate in Olympic weightlifting competitions, and travel the world; some of his doctors would give you a resounding no. But they had never met our dad, and they had never seen what his boots could do.

I admire that our dad always let us into his fears about his cancer. That we had so many conversations about how difficult it was. There were times when he and I would just sit together and lament all the things that he would have to watch from the sky. We'd talk about the obvious big stuff, but also the little things. like how I'd miss getting a "luv u" text during the day, or a picture of me that he loved. He would miss the days that we got, just the five of us.

But most of all, he told me that he would miss our mom. God, our dad loved our mom. They loved hard, and man they fought hard. Part of his story, as you all know, is that he was an incredibly stubborn and persistent man. Lucky for him, he married an incredibly stubborn woman. Ron, Zach, and I watched them do this dance for their twenty-six years of marriage. When they would fight, neither would back down, and they let each other know that they weren't going too, loudly. Very loudly. But then, they would take a beat and a breath, and they would get quieter and quieter until they found each other again.

This dance of marriage included his favorite time of day, 4:50 am when he would hit snooze on his alarm clock, get back in bed, and snuggle with my mom. Craig Laurence Kruse loved Kristen Beth Kruse like it was breathing. Sometimes, it was something he did without thinking. Other times, it was labored, hard, and difficult. But he didn't stop until his final breath, and to be honest I don't even think he did after that. He met the love of his life at eighteen and made every second count.

I guess that's living, isn't it: loving with absolutely everything you've got? Loving people so much and so hard that you are more upset about what your dying will to do them rather than the death itself. Our dad showed Ron, Zach, and me that love is messy, imperfect, and vulnerable. It's hard, but it's worth everything. Craig Kruse was a scary-looking dude, but man he loved the hell out of his people

He always told me that the hardest part of all of this was leaving us too soon. and we felt it. In the end, he was the most upset about how sad the four of us would be when he was gone. He was honest about how he just wanted to take this all away from us, that he was so sorry his cancer would bring sadness into our lives that would never go away.

Life is hard. Life is painful. Life is messy. but to avoid these things, to live in a pain-free way, our dad taught us that isn't living at all. He had the chance to succumb to it all, to wallow in pain or deny it altogether. Instead, he put his boots on. He had the courage to live, and to leave a mark on this world that lasts far beyond his last breath.

In his book, "A Grief Observed" C.S. Lewis talks about how the deeper the love, the deeper the grief. Our Grandma George echoed the same sentiment to me often, she told me that I wouldn't be so sad if I didn't care so much. Our dad's cancer trek was impossibly difficult. It was the twilight zone, the perpetual state of saying goodbye. And while I often wanted to shrink away, he never did. I believe that he knew deep in his bones that this was the cost of love, terribly and impossibly hard goodbyes. But he would tell you, the love is worth a hundred times over.

There are many of you here today who have healed bodies because of him, he left a tangible mark on your life by using his hands and his words to help you. There are also many of you here who got better at a sport you love because of him. He left a mark on your life by teaching you how to throw a shot put or block in football. But then are those of us, his closest friends and his family, who will forever be touched by the littlest of things. The way he laughed, his love of carrot cake and key lime pie, and how his love and constant care felt. His love was consistent, visible, and tangible. He always told the people he loved what they meant to him. He left nothing unsaid or unknown.

He had the courage to live.

I'm grateful for the pieces of him that we will always have. The shape of Zach's feet, the way that Ron laughs, and the men that they are and will grow into being. For our blonde eyebrows, that always let everyone know that we were his. But most of all, I'm grateful that his heart, work ethic, sense of humor, and the best of him, he left behind two incredible men who will carry on the Kruse name well.

There are a million more things that I could say about this wonderful man. That one time he came to pick me up from cross country practice in high school, all the windows of his car down, blasting Sweet Caroline and laughing at the top of his lungs. Or how when we were kids my mom worked on Saturdays and that meant we stayed with our dad and did three things, ate the food in the fridge that was about to go bad, went to Bass Pro Shops, and got temporary tattoos. Every. Single. Saturday.

I wish I could tell you about all of the stories that we got the privilege of hearing over the years, his adventures as a kid, his escapades at Augie, and every life lesson he ever learned. I wish I could show you how much our dad did live.

But instead, I leave you with this, we honor our dad in the coming years, in the ones that he will not reside on this side of heaven, by the way, that we live, why we live, and who we live for.

We live in an honest way. We show up for work with a smile on our faces, do things when we aren't asked, and always go the extra mile.

We book the flights, take the trips, lean in for the kiss, and take the leap. We go for it because he always did.

We also apologize, both when we are wrong and when we want to heal the relationship. And more than anything, we tell our people that we love them and that we are proud of them. Because we knew that our dad was proud of all of us, it was just a fact. He said it all the time, and never let us forget it.

We live for God, for good values, and for the people around us. We remember that in whatever area we work, whoever we interact with, we are the hands and feet of Jesus. We show up because it's what's right. After all, it's the loving thing to do, and because we get to. We put our boots on because he showed us how.

We marry kind people, befriend the ones who need it, and always lend a helping hand.

We make our presence one that is missed. We have the courage to live. And we choose to hope; because hope does not change our reality but instead changes us.

Knowing him, he'd want me to leave you all with a quote. My dad got the phrase "Boots On" from a movie our family watches at our lake house called Second Hand Lions. One of the main characters, Uncle Hub, says at one point in the movie that dying with your boots on means dying doing what you love, dying while living. We watched the movie a couple of days after we found out about his diagnosis last year, and he heard that line again, and said to us, "Yeah, that's it. Exactly." But, that was never my favorite part of the movie, nor my favorite thing that Uncle Hub said. Later in the movie, he gives a speech to his young great-nephew, Walter.

He says "There's a long speech I give to young men and it seems like you need to hear a piece of it. Just a piece. Sometimes, the things that may or may not be true are the things that a man needs to believe in the most. That people are basically good. That honor, courage and virtue mean everything. That power and money, money and power, mean nothing. That good always triumphs over evil. And I want you to remember this, that love, true love, never dies. You remember that boy, you remember that. Doesn't matter if it's true or not you see, a man should believe in those things because those are the things worth believing in. Got that?"

Our dad made those things true for us. His love, the love he poured into his work, his coaching, and his people, will never die.

Dad, I know that you are probably up in heaven teaching Jesus and Paul proper squat form, and maybe that's why they took you from us too soon. But thank you. Thank you for being a man that has too many good qualities and memories to fit into a eulogy. Thank you for showing all of us what it means to be brave, and that it means living a life that is honest and filled with love. Thank you for marrying the right girl, and giving Ron, Zach, and me an incredible mom. Thank you for showing your kids what deep, meaningful love in marriage looks like. Thank you for giving us a community filled to the brim with good people.

But most of all, thank you for being our dad. We will never move on from this grief. Instead, we move forward, both with it and with you. And you equipped us for this because of how you loved us. We will continue to make you proud. Luv u.

Rewritten Eulogy

September 20, 2022

I began writing my dad's eulogy shortly after we found out about his cancer. I know that sounds a little neurotic because it is.

I didn't tell anyone until just before he passed away, but I had been writing and rewriting for over a year. Part of it was expressing my love for him over and over again was a really valuable way for me to cope with what was going on. Another part was I believed he deserved the very best of my writing, and that was going to take a while. And some of it, though I wouldn't admit it at the time, was that I thought if I could read him this before he died that it would make up for all the things I would never get to tell him.

One day during undergrad, I looked at myself in the mirror and realized that there was nothing that I had ever done that I was truly proud of. I always had a weird internal reaction when my parents, coaches, or friends would tell me that they were proud of me. I always knew that I had more in me and that I had never given anything my full, honest, 100% effort. Admittedly, I was being a little harsh on myself. But I always wondered what it felt like to know that you had given absolutely everything. I looked back at my cross country meets and that I had run a little slower than I needed to because I was scared I wouldn't have enough energy to finish. Or wondered what would have happened if I had been even just a little more consistent in the gym, on the court, or on the field. I wondered if I would have been able to handle harder classes, a harder major, or a different school.

And it's not that I was lazy, nor that I didn't try. It's that everything got about 90% effort on my end, and I always knew that in the back of my head. To me, that wasn't worth being proud of.

But as I steadied my shaking voice during his funeral, quickly wiping my tears after saying his full name, I knew that this eulogy had gotten every part of me. If I had to deliver it today, I really don't think I would have the emotional fortitude to be able to. But it was not even a question for me then. I felt that he deserved this from me. Maybe the public speaking classes, the Caring Bridge posts, and all the reading that I had done were carrying me to this moment. Maybe most things in life only get 90% from you because very, very few things deserve 100%.

I don't know, most people may disagree with that sentiment, but I know I could not have shown up for my dad how he needed me to if I was showing up perfectly for everyone and everything else. Rather than giving everything 100% of our effort, I have settled on the idea that we only have 100% to give. If you give all of yourself to your job, you have nothing left for the people you love. If your sport gets all of your attention, the school won't. If your boyfriend does, your friends won't.

But this eulogy? It got 100% of me over the year I wrote it, snowballing to that the closer it got to its completion. How do you succinctly eulogize someone? How do you memorialize them while just beginning to navigate life without them? Honestly, I think I did this well because I sucked at a lot of other stuff. While finishing writing his eulogy the week after he passed, I was not showing up fully anywhere else. Granite, I was one week into grieving my dad. But nothing got more attention from me than this. I let myself be bad at a million other things so I could give my dad something from me I believed that he deserved.

Last month, when I was filling out scholarship applications for graduate school, I was asked to name the accomplishment I was most proud of. I told them about this, about how eulogizing my dad was the most important thing I had ever done. I don't think I will come close to it for a long time, and I think that is okay. Maybe it's okay if I go back to giving everything 90% of me, maybe even less. Maybe the 100% are reserved for eulogies, for births, and deaths. Maybe we only show up fully when we have no other choice, and maybe it's okay to half-ass things that don't deserve anything more from us.

Moving On

September 27, 2022

When I watched some of my peers lose their dads, I was always shocked at how soon they went back to "normal". How they accepted their life, what had happened, and then just, came back. I remember watching a close friend lose her dad and being astounded by her because she was okay. I remember thinking to myself "Well if that happened to me, I think that I would just lose my mind".

Well, here I am, and I haven't lost it. Granted, we are only just over three weeks out. For all, we know when I hit six months I will have a break from reality and just go off the deep end. But if I were a betting man, I would say I will be here, in okay land, for a long time.

I see it in my friend's eyes, this astonishment that I once held. I hear it in my boyfriend when after laughing together he draws out a "so…" because he doesn't want to ask me how I am.

Because duh. I feel it in the extra-long hugs I'm still getting. It's like people are saying "Okay, drop the act".

And the worst part is, I wish I was acting. I wish it still felt fresh and unbearable like it did when we first found out my dad was sick. When I had to go on hours-long walks to stop myself from crying so hard that I vomited. Instead, this pain is now just a part of me. It's no longer shocking, but instead just reality.

I wish I could tell myself that people move on because their loss just becomes a part of them. I sent my boyfriend a video of my dad the other day, and he asked "What made you decide to send this". Very much in a "drop the act" way, though very lovingly. I think he thought that something he had said had made me think of my dad, and he didn't want to upset me. But I told him, I'm never not thinking about my dad.

I'm at the point of grieving where I just want to talk about normal life and normal things. But it's not because I'm avoiding the pain. It's that I spend so much time there, just sitting in it, that my dad comes with me everywhere now. I think about him when

I'm not thinking about him. I smell him, I hear his laugh, I feel his breath. It's this part of my life that I can only verbalize a small piece of because the rest is so sacred that it doesn't fit into vocabulary.

I love talking about the parts of him that made me laugh. He always used to tell me that I smelled like runny dog shit. Sometimes, he would even text me "RDS", with no explanation. So the other day, when I took our dog Boots on a walk, and I had to pick up my first runny dog shit, I knew that he was definitely having a field day.

I guess I thought that when someone this important in your life dies, everything just implodes. I wouldn't have put it in those words, but I think deep down I thought that once my dad was gone that everything would change. And I'm not saying it hasn't been hard, nor am I saying that my life hasn't changed. But, it didn't fall apart. He is still my rock, even when he isn't physically here to be it.

But really, that means he did his job as my dad. My life didn't implode because he taught me how to live without him. He taught me that pain will not break me. I thought that when he died that grieving would take over my entire life. I would envision myself just locking my bedroom door, closing the blinds, and laying in bed for weeks. Instead, I walked downstairs, sat down in the living room every morning, and just showed up as honestly as I could.

I think what I'm learning is that people never truly die. He is still such a part of me, and my life. He is my favorite story to tell, I'm just so sad that there is an ending.

Okay

October 5, 2022

I worry that I'm too okay.

I almost question if I am numb to what happened, even though I am not. I cognitively know that I have felt this every step of the way. I remember the night I found out what this diagnosis meant, and how I sat over my toilet in the dark for hours just dry heaving. Or having to leave class at the drop of a dime because I felt suffocated by my emotions. Or the day he was diagnosed with pneumonia, and I walked outside of work, crumbled to the ground, and sobbed into my boyfriend's arms. Or, for that matter, the 417 days that this was my dad's reality. I remember all of it.

But now? Why am I okay now? Why do I go days without crying about him? Why do I think of him, and smile? Why is this not killing me?

In the weeks leading up to my dad's passing, I would talk to him about what signs he would give us. I asked him to be loud because I was afraid I was going to miss them or pretend like everything that happened was him. But, as he declined, while he slept, I continually asked him if he would visit my dreams. I told him that I needed to make sure that he was doing okay, and that was the best place to do it. I also knew, in my heart of hearts, that God would let us have this. That even if it was just once, He would provide this.

The day he passed away, I prayed to God that I could see my dad in my dream that night. I did. So I prayed again, and I saw him again. I didn't interact with him either time, but I just got to see him, standing up. But, they were still dreams. I didn't know at that moment that he was gone, and I ended up just sobbing when I woke up because I would never get to talk to him again.

Then, a couple of weeks ago, I had this unexplainable dream. I was playing in a rec league game and I saw my dad come in with a folding chair. He was wearing this heavy green jacket that he has owned my entire life, black basketball shorts, white socks that were pulled up just a little too high, and his orange and gray New Balance shoes. It was him. I walked up to him, and I knew he was in Heaven, and that he had come to visit me.

Neither of us cried or truly acted like anything was out of the ordinary. I just squeezed him tight, kissed him on the forehead, and went to turn around to walk onto the court. But then I paused and turned back around. I locked eyes with him, and I asked him if Heaven was going okay. He looked at me, smiled and nodded with these knowing eyes that I have known all of my life.

A couple of days ago I was walking in from the garage and happened to look to my left. There, I saw his green jacket. I grabbed it, and it felt just like it had in my dream. It was a feeling beyond knowing, it was the feeling of home.

Now you may not believe me, and that's okay. I don't know where this dream fits in with my theology. But I do know that God has used dreams to communicate before, so I thought I would ask Him to do it again. I will tell you, I think that maybe, this dream may be why I'm okay right now.

This look he gave me, was like he was trying to communicate to me how little I know about where he is right now. He had this soft smile on his face like he was saying "Oh Cassie, I couldn't even explain it if I tried". I know he is okay. That he is just basking in the fullness of Christ, and that he knows everything I have gotten right and wrong about God.

I think I knew he came to visit me, and that this wasn't just a dream, because it was like he just walked into a dream I was already having. It was so random, and then he was just there. And who knows, maybe this is just me coping. But if it is, is that so bad? Is I having a dream that I believe to be my dad communicating with me from the Great Beyond to tell me that he is okay, is it that bad if I believe that to be true?

I think this dream helped me realize that his time on Earth is done. That he isn't coming back, and that that is okay. Truthfully, I think he is having a much better time than any of us are having, and I wouldn't wish him back here from the joy he is experiencing.

I'm still sad. I'm still angry that his life had to end when his kids' was just beginning. I'm in shock that I have attended my own father's funeral. But, I am not overcome by it. I may be too okay, and my boat may be rocked soon. But, I think I'm okay because I do believe that he is.

Becoming

November 10, 2022

I've been reading a lot more. I finally bit the bullet and decided to try audiobooks. In my snobby college ways, part of me didn't think that counted as reading for a long time. It's been six days and I've already read a whole book, and am making my way through two more. I started working out again, lifting. I haven't been running, but I've been taking our dog Boots on my favorite four-mile loop every chance I get. I started working again. I am in my second week of a job I love. I see my boyfriend every chance I get and talk to my closest friends almost every day.

I'm becoming. I'm making my way to the woman that I will be without my dad. For the last two months of his life, and the month after, I could not think of her. Instead, I sat in the girl I was. The girl that my dad had known. I would sit and just live in our past. In all of the wonderful memories that he has given me. And while this type of coping has its place, and it's a beautiful and necessary place, I can not live my life simply reminiscing on the first twenty-two years of it.

I am becoming, because of who I was. I am becoming, because of who my dad was, and I am becoming because of all that he wanted me to be.

Megan Markle

November 12, 2022

I have been reading Brené Brown's *Atlas of the Heart*, her newest book. Brown is one of my favorite authors, and possibly one of my favorite public figures. She is a shame researcher, and her work has a lot to do with this art of becoming. This piece of her work is her attempt at a map of human emotions, where she pooled together her favorite researchers to better define the different things we all feel. She did this so that we may be better able to pinpoint what is really going on in our hearts and our minds, and so to maybe lessen the space of miscommunication.

This work helped me realize how much resentment I have been holding onto. Brown talked about how you know you are in resentment when you are rehearsing what you want to say to someone.

Ouch.

It's when you are having an imaginary fight, and you are perfecting exactly how you can get your message across, and how to get a few digs in there, too. I saw how I was doing this with everyone in my life, with my mom especially.

My mom, like any good mom, is my safe space. She, more than anyone else in my life, has always gotten the most unfiltered version of me. She was the one who witnessed all of my fits in my terrible twos, bore me through some rough moments in my teenage years, and every hard moment in between. She bore witness to and stuck by me through the worst parts of myself.

When I was growing up, fighting was an hours-long ordeal. When one of my parents and I would get into a spat (yes, I was the sibling who fought with our parents every chance I got), neither of us could let it go. So we had this cycle, where we would yell and scream and stomp around at each other. Then, we would calm down. Now my mom and I, we always wanted to sit in this place. We wanted to go to bed, to talk about what we were disagreeing about in the morning. But we never, ever could, because then my dad would start the hours-long reconciliation discussion. Where the three of us would sit in their room and talk through what we were really *actually* mad about.

Now in some ways, this isn't great. Life's deepest issues are not things you can solve together in one night. This led my mom and me to table some things until our next showdown, just so that we could be done and my dad could rest easy. But, it did bite resentment in the butt in a lot of ways. It often felt that these discussions were a no-holds-bar. A place where I did not have to worry about their feelings (and often did not care to). Somewhere where they could tell me my deepest faults, and also a place where we could try and see where the other one was coming from.

Many of our fights happened because the three of us were ridiculously stubborn. I do believe that is the danger of marrying someone with a similar fault to your own, you can make a kid who has that issue, squared. Without my dad in these showdowns, my mom and I began to sit in the calm, not talking about deeper things. Then I found myself, for obvious reasons, not wanting to fight with her. But you see, I was not choosing to let go of things in favor of peace. No, I was just burying them.

When you have a sick family member, everything becomes stressful and 97% of it is not stuff that feels worth addressing. In the last couple of months of my dad's life, he ended up needing to go to the hospital for a multiple-day stay literally every single week. He was treated at Northwestern, which we loved, but it was an hour's commute most days, both ways. This wore all of us down, eroded our compassion for each other, and sharpened our edges. I began to build up my resentment stash, subconsciously waiting for my chance to fire them on an unsuspecting one of them.

Then one day, my mom and I fought when we got home. We were watching the news when she started to talk about how annoying she found Megan Markle.

Now, there is some history here. My mom and I have never agreed on this (in my opinion) wonderful lady. She and her whole side of the family are big Royal family fans, while I have always had more of an understanding of the Mountbatten-Windsor couple. And we have gotten into our fair share of spats about it. But, it was never anything that serious.

Yes, I am about to tell you a story about a knockdown, drag-out, fight I had with my mom about Megan Markle.

She started talking about the things about Markle that bothered her, and I shot back. What she did not know is that while she was trying to just let off some steam, I was readying my stash of resentment. I had months worth of things that I wanted to get off my chest, and I finally had the opportunity to unleash them onto her. This fight lasted for hours, and it was one in that we unleashed every hurtful thing we had thought about each other while sitting together within those hospital walls.

We didn't have my dad there to end it. He wasn't there to separate us, to use his booming voice to his advantage to stop both of us for a second. We had full reign to deeply hurt the person who arguably deserved it the least from us.

Shauna Niequist wrote about showing the worst of ourselves to our favorite people in her book *Present over Perfect*. She writes,

"It's easy to be liked by strangers.

It's very hard to be loved and connected to the people in your home

when you're always bringing them your most exhausted self

and resenting the fact that the scraps you're giving them aren't cutting it."

The first time I read these words, they stung familiarly. Like this was something that I knew in my soul, but had not known the words to. In a normal situation, my family was getting my scraps. My teammates, roommates, professors, and pastors were getting the best of me. But in cancer, everyone gets the scraps. And that means that your family, they at times get almost nothing.

Now, I won't be too dramatic here. I do believe that our family handled our dad's cancer the best way that we could. We did show up for each other and took care of one another in our ways. But on the hard days, the days that we were commuting an hour to sit in a hospital room with our sick dad, that's when we couldn't spare each other anything. Those were the days that rather than letting things go, I buried things deep. Those were the days when my loved ones could not even get the scraps from me.

It was interesting to know these things while walking someone to Eternity. Our mom started a Caring Bridge blog when our dad first got sick. Throughout his trek, he, my mom, and I would write posts on there. This was the place where I finally started making my writings public. This is also the place I venture back to, from time to time, to read our dad's words. When he wrote about his fears, his highs, and his lows. But the thing that I have been going back to recently was how much he talked about how deeply he loved our mom and my brothers.

May 9, 2022

Well.... tomorrow will be here whether I want it to be or not. This is the most anxious I have been about a scan. I do not have a very good feeling about it.

I appreciate all of my friends and family texting and writing emails letting us know they are praying for us. Because of my strong faith, I truly believe the results tomorrow have already been determined. I wish extra prayers or a positive attitude could help with the scan tomorrow. Instead of praying for a positive scan tomorrow, please pray for me to have the strength to deal with whatever the outcome is for the sake of Kristen, Cass, Ron, and Zach. That is my biggest fear... that I will not be strong enough for them. This is harder than I thought it could ever be...Please pray for me to be strong for them...

Love everyone,

Craig

During his trek, our dad tried his very best to never give us his scraps. While there were hard times and fights, I now see him making an effort to give us the best of him. Part of me wishes I could have modeled myself after him better during this time, but I also have a lot of grace for all of us.

But, we did find our way back to each other. It took a lot longer than it usually did, and there was no hours-long reconciliation conversation. Instead, I looked at her and said "I don't think I was mad at you about Megan Markle", and she laughed, agreeing.

Before reading Brown's work, I would not have been able to pinpoint that I had been building resentment toward my closest family members. It makes sense, we tend to be our fullest, ugliest selves around people that we know will not leave us. But, that does not mean they deserve that side of us. This ugliness, while it does not result in leaving, does bread its form of long-term consequences.

After understanding that it was resentment that I was feeling, I was a little crushed. While to some extent some of my frustrations were warranted, I looked at my mom and asked myself why I thought she did not deserve my forgiveness. Why did she not get the benefit of the doubt from me, why could I not just let her off the hook sometimes? Why in the world would she be the person that I am holding resentment towards?

I'm afraid I am my shittiest self to my favorite people.

I hold resentment towards my mom because she is the person that I have gone through the ugliest of stuff with. I also realized that I hold so much resentment toward her because I expect her to be perfect. I never really got to that stage of young adulthood where you saw your parents as people. She was, and will always be my hero. The bad part of that is when she isn't heroic when she is human, I am doubly crushed.

So I get mad at her about Megan Markle, when she asks me to put the dishes away, and when she can't bring my dad back to life. I get mad at her when my insides feel hot and she can't stop them. When she is the only person in my life that understands me, and yet feels a million miles away. When she is a widow and not just my mom.

Mr. Jim

December 29, 2022

My dad met Mr. Jim during his sophomore year of college. Mr. Jim had transferred as a junior, and my dad's roommate was a friend of his in high school. So this roommate invited Mr. Jim to sit with them at lunch, and the rest is history. In the 22 years that I was around the two of them, I never saw them disagree about one thing. When he was our next-door neighbor, I used to joke that our dad would get a "Mr. Jim" face, in which his face would always light up around his best friend, no matter how much the rest of his life was frustrating him. Their friendship was one of joy, of shouldering each other's burdens, of brotherhood.

That's why my brothers and I call him Mr. Jim. Mr. Zajieck was much too formal for Ron's Godfather, but I think my dad would have keeled over if we had called an adult by their first name before we were one ourselves. So, Mr. Jim, it was, and Mr. Jim it will always be.

I asked him about his favorite memory with my dad, and he couldn't give me a straight answer. Instead, he walked me through some of the best parts of their friendship. How when they were both young professionals, they didn't want to spend a lot of money going out. So they would go see a movie, sneak around the theatre after it ended to see one or two more, and then go to Denny's afterward. He laughed, remarking how that isn't the idea of fun for most other late twenty-something-year-old men. But for them? It was perfect.

Mr. Jim built our house and was the one we called whenever anything went wrong. My dad wasn't exactly the handiest of people, but it was okay because he had his best friend. Even now, he is always just one call away. He loves my mom, and brothers and I like we are his own because in a way we are. We belong to our people, and they belong to us. I have never met two men who belonged to each other more than Mr. Jim and my dad. So even when my dad is not here, Mr. Jim is still ours, and we are his.

For a long time, I never understood why people called close family friends aunts or uncles. Because while I obviously love my family, Mr. Jim was so much more than that for my dad. He was a brother in the best ways, without any of the hard parts. He was in a safe space. Somebody who did not expect or need anything from my dad. Somebody who saw the world from his point of view, and somebody to hold the weight of his problems in a way that none of the rest of us could.

When my dad was near the end of his life, Mr. Jim was one of the only other people who got it. He didn't need to tell us about how much our dad had impacted him, because we all just knew. Instead, he would come over, sit with us, and just tell us the stupidest stories to make us laugh.

He was holding the weight of our dad's death, in a way none of the rest of us could. And, he never made it about himself. There are a million ways that other people made grieving my dad more difficult, but Mr. Jim? He did what a best friend should do, he just showed up.

Mr. Jim will be the man to walk me down the aisle. He will be the man that Ron and Zach go to when they need fatherly advice. He will be the one watching over my mom when the three of us move out and away. He is so much more than a best friend. He is our Mr. Jim, and it is as simple as that.

Yes, my dad only got 50 years here, and yes, it was all in all incredibly and devastatingly too short. But he got a Kristen Kruse and a Mr. Jim. And maybe that was enough. Maybe it's enough because it has to be.

I Love You. So Much.

January 28, 2023

I love you.

I love you.

So much.

So much.

You're my favorite dad.

You're my favorite daughter.

    I began this repetition back and forth with my dad when he came home on hospice. I still couldn't tell you exactly why, I think part of me just wanted to continue to make special memories with him until his very last breath. We said it to each other numerous times a day, though I always had to start it. It was also a little check-in with him, just for me. I knew that once he couldn't remember it anymore, he was really leaving us.

    He never forgot.

Even when he could no longer open his eyes when he was sleeping for a week straight. Sometimes, I would say it, and he would whisper it back to me. Though he had a tumor invading his brain from all sides, it could never steal him away from us. He wasn't the tumor's to take. He was fully, completely, ours, to his very last breath and even now.

I see him in everything. I hear him in the verbiage that comes spilling out of my mouth sometimes, words and phrases that I learned from him. I see him in every sunset and every sunrise, especially the ones that are extra orange. I feel his heartbeat pulsing through each of my family members. I've now seen that death is not the worst thing that can happen to you, it is living a life without love.

God, that is cheesy, but it is true. The love he left here for us, and the love he sends every day, helps me to not be bitter. Because I can not think of anything worse, or anything that would have made him angrier than me letting his death ruin my life. I grieve for him with the hope that I will see him again someday, and that I need to have a good life to report back on.

I've seen the idea floating around that although your departed parent can not be with you in the future, they are the reason you will be who you will become. My dad will not meet my children. That always has been, and probably always will be, devastating to me.

But, he will still teach them so much. He will help me show them hard work, confidence, and strength. He will help me teach them about the preserving, all-consuming, power of love. I will tell them of their wonderful grandpa, and how he lived an authentic life until the very end.

I can not wait to tell them of this moment, this phrase, this repetition. How he didn't leave me, didn't leave us, even when everything was pulling him away.

I love you.

I love you.

So much.

So much.

You're my favorite dad.

You're my favorite daughter.

Faith

January 29, 2023

In October of 2021, my dad decided against a treatment plan that I wanted him to do, one that I was convinced would keep him here longer. I left class, texted my pastor, and asked him to meet me at church. That was one good thing about grieving while a senior in college, this did take precedents. People just understood, and let me leave when I needed to leave. When I got to church, my pastor was sitting there, strumming along on his guitar with a warm cup of coffee in front of him.

I started attending this church my freshman year when my faith was still shiny, new, and unchallenged. Truthfully, I started attending because of the vibe. It gave off the "hippie and trendy" feeling that I wanted after attending a traditional ELCA Lutheran church my entire life. At the time, I was not looking at theology, or who they employed. I had not bothered to ask if they were affirming or if women were a part of the leadership team. I did not know how important these things were to me until I got there and saw them in action.

While I came for the vibes and aesthetics, I stayed because my faith was allowed to be whatever it needed to be here. After working at a Bible camp one summer I came back to school absolutely on fire for the Lord, and they plugged me into serving. When I was having a really hard time in my junior year they would feed me dinner and take me out for coffee. This was and is the type of church that took me as I was and did not ask me to change.

That is why I felt safe enough to go to my pastor on one of the hardest days of my life. My faith was falling apart. I did not know how to believe in a God that was not going to fix this. Worse, I literally could not stand to be around other Christians who talked about how God had shown up for them that week by helping them find their car keys.

All in all, I was pissed at God.

And I couldn't find the answers from my people. My mom was just as mad as I was. My roommates were not as tied down to their faith as I was, and my dad did not blame God. I felt like I was out on an island in the middle of the ocean, screaming into the abyss. It felt even weirder to be this mad at God on my dad's behalf when he wasn't. He never asked "Why me" or got angry. He had the type of faith and trust in God where he just accepted what God gave him, come what may.

I wanted more from Him. Looking back, I didn't even want a miracle, I wanted Him to turn back time. I wanted Him to give this to me instead because to me the pain of possibility could not be as bad as the pain of losing someone like my dad. Someone who did so much good for the people around him, who cared so deeply, and who loved so much. I wanted to turn back time and get to choose who got this cancer, and just take it instead.

I found out my dad had a seizure and was in the hospital in this church. I was an intern that summer, and I was there by myself doing some work on uploading audio files. I went to the bathroom and was standing in the stall when my mom called me.

"Okay I have to tell you something I don't want you to freak out and I don't want you to drive up here". We did not know yet what was going on, nor how bad it was. All we knew is that I do not take bad news well, and my mom was trying to care for me from 200 miles away.

Here I was, again, standing in this church, processing horrible news, again. And yet, I had chosen to come back here. Because even though I would not admit it at the time, I was angry at God because I loved Him so much. It was less shaking my fist at an apathetic Creator and so much more pleading for my Heavenly Father to rescue me.

My pastor hugged me, and then just listened to me. He did not open his Bible and point me to passages of God being faithful, nor of God being kind of mean to other people, too. He just listened and cried with me. He told me of his love for his kids, and how he would want them to use their faith if something happened to him. After, he told me that this was a conversation that God and I needed to have, just us two. He gave me the keys and told me to take as long as I needed and to let God know exactly what was going on in my heart.

"He can handle it, I promise". He said with a hug, and then left me alone in the church lobby.

I took a deep breath and then opened the doors to the sanctuary. I walked to the back, laid down, and just sobbed. Truthfully, I only remember my anger in this conversation. I told God that He needed to fuck off and leave my dad the fuck alone. I screamed at how cruel this all was, and I told him that there was no way that He needed my dad as much as we did. I was there alone, just God and I, for a long time. Eventually, my breathing evened out, I felt the fiery anger die down a little, and I got up and left.

Later that night, while praying in my bed, I did apologize for the expletives, don't worry. What I learned on this day, the day that I told God He needed to fuck off, was that my faith did not need to explain this away. I was looking for an answer that just does not exist. I realized that to get through losing my dad, I needed to let Him in.

I have gone through an interesting journey in my faith, especially considering I am only 23. There was a period in my life when everything was spiritual. When I had no personality besides being a Christian. When I didn't let myself be a human being, be a young adult, be a person with feelings and doubts. Then, when that person hurt too much, I put everything down. And in many ways, this part of my faith journey is something I am extremely proud of. I began to read about church history and learn about other people's experiences. I learned that this God that I believed in, this Jesus that I loved, this Holy Spirit that lived inside me, wasn't asking me to suffer on Their behalf. For so long I had thought that dying to oneself and picking up your cross meant accepting the miserable parts of life, and just soldier on. So, when hard things happened, I just thought that God was calling me to have a good attitude in the storm.

Then, my dad got sick. And rather than dying to myself, I saw that there was a lot of suffering I was saying yes to that I just had to walk away from. I learned that perhaps dying to myself was realizing that I was a human being, and it was wrong to just try to be the best Christian possible. Perhaps dying to yourself and picking up your cross meant not giving up.

And sometimes, not giving up meant saying no so that you could say yes. I needed to say yes to being fully present with my dad during his illness. I had to have the mental capacity to deal with all that it would entail. I knew that there would never be anything more important to show up fully for. And so, many of the things that were in my life simply to die to myself, I finally let them go.

I do not think that if I was still in my overly spiritual state that I would have survived my dad's trek in the way that I did. Sure, that girl never would have sat in a church sanctuary and screamed obscenities at God. That girl also had a problem with being real. She probably would have put all her stock in her dad being healed, rather than being in the present moment and just being honest. There are many reasons I am incredibly grateful for how my parents handled this, but one of the best was how real they both were about it. I would not have survived without their honesty.

The year before my dad got sick, I was almost surveying my faith, not fully tied to it. I was angry about some of the experiences that I had had, the way many Christians dealt with social and political issues, and how I felt that the type of faith I had separated me from those I loved most. I had put my faith down, but still had my hand on it.

I had a hard time picking my faith back up because it was much more fragmented than when I put it down. I believed in God, but I didn't know if He was loving. I knew that Jesus was walking with my family through this, but I did not know if I was okay with where He was leading. I knew that the Holy Spirit dwelled in me, but I questioned why It was so silent.

Truth be told, my faith is still fragmented. I have watched different pieces fuse, and different pieces fall off entirely. I don't know if I would call this process "deconstruction" for me, simply because I had so many positive experiences in my faith that I have been finding my way back to. But, I also feel I have deconstructed and walked away from many harmful things I picked up along the way. I feel like when people talk about questioning their faith and being angry at Christianity, many can be scared or turned off. However, I think that if faith and religious institutions are important, they are worth questioning.

The faith I had before I put it down was adverse to pain. It could not handle questions, doubt, or fear. It was a faith of "God does not give you more than you can handle" and "everything happens for a reason". Though I miss some parts of that faith, the certainty, and the unceasing joy, I am grateful to have a faith that has been forged and molded by the fire. Because while the fire can kill and destroy, Shadrach, Meshach, and Abednego tell us

that there is Another in the fire with us.[1]

---

[1] The story of Shadrach, Meshach, and Abednego appears in Daniel 3. The three are sentenced to die in the furnace by King Nebuchadnezzar because they will not worship his golden idol. They come out unharmed, and the guards see another in there with them. Many, including myself, believe this to be a story of how God never leaves us, no matter the circumstance.

Mess

April 14, 2023

Here's what I know.

The first thing we do when we begin our lives is cry. A blood-curdling scream cry that takes all the gunk out of our lungs and lets everyone know that we made it here okay. Before we open our eyes, we cry. It's how we come alive.

I know that as a baby that is the only way that we can communicate. Before we smile, laugh, or speak, we cry. We cry when we are hungry when we need to be changed, and when we have an itch we can't scratch. When there is fuzz between our toes, a sudden noise, and when we think we've been abandoned.

And then, somewhere along the way, we learn that this is the worst way to communicate. We learn we must use words. That crying inconveniences the people around you, and it's only okay when you are cute enough for everyone to stomach it.

Here's what I also know.

I've cried that cry, the cry to clear the gunk out of your lungs, the cry that lets everyone know you are alive, many times over the last two years. I cried like that after my dad's first surgery when he and I walked around the hospital wing and he gave me instructions on how to care for everyone else when he was gone. When I went on a nine-mile walk and screamed about how my dad was going to miss everything. When Zach had his first big meet without him, when Ron moved back to school, and when our mom got the kitchen redone.

I know that one of those days, in those moments, was the only thing reminding me that I was alive.

I did not cry like that at his wake, his funeral, or when I gave his eulogy. Not when we buried some of his ashes, when I speak of him, nor when I look at my grandpa and I finally see how similar they look. Because in those moments, I did not need to be reminded that I was alive. I felt it in his absence, in the presence of his memory, and in the responsibility, I felt to mourn him with dignity and grace.

I know that if doctors do not hear this gunk-clearing cry, they immediately get worried. If you come into the world silently, it means you aren't fully here yet. Part of me wonders if I wasn't fully present in this world until I cried like this as an adult. I have found for myself true empathy.

In C.S. Lewis's book *The Magician's Nephew*, Aslan, the character who is meant to represent God, is speaking to the only other person in all of Narnia that truly understands grief.

" *'My son, My son,' said Aslan.*

'I know. Grief is great, only you and I in this land know that yet.

Let us be good to one another.'"

This response from God, accompanied by tears and the inability (for whatever reason) to do something, speaks deeply to me. God was the first to weep when my dad was diagnosed, even though He knew from the very beginning that this was what would happen. He wept with us because He loves and understands us.

I know that this is not something that I believed for a long, long time. Even now, I know it is faith and hope alone that lead me to this conclusion. Aslan speaking this truth also hit me so deeply because I was getting mad at my mom about Megan Markle, at Ron and Zach for also being deeply upset and angry, and at my dad for dying. Grief is so isolating that sometimes you forget that other people are going through it, too.

I know that grief erupted in parts of myself, both that I loved and hated. I know that I am not the same person I was when I had a healthy dad. I know that nobody who loved him is, either.

I know that grief brings out the best and the worst in people, which is why I need the reminder to be good to those who get it. I know that sometimes, people show up for you poorly. I know that some people can not handle the blood-curdling scream and that they would prefer to just see the birth announcement. I know that some people want to be there for the pictures, but not for the hard stuff. I know that people will make death about themselves. For most, true empathy can not be taught, but instead simply understood.

In my dad's eulogy, I spoke a lot about love. When I was looking back at his life, I knew this was the greatest lesson that he taught me. How to love deeply, truly, and fully. I spoke about how he showed me that above all else, life and love if done well, are messy.

After these last two years, the Sacred Year, and the year to follow, I am grateful for the mess. My best friend Kate has this saying, "sit in the mess", that has meant a lot to me since we met. It is the reminder I always needed, that life is not meant to fit into the boxes we always seem so desperate to fit into. But these last two years? I finally understand that the mess is also loud. Mess is coming into this world, covered in gunk, screaming and crying to announce your presence. It is allowing yourself to sink deep into the abyss of despair, only to discover that there is a bottom, you just had to let yourself get there.

As I look back on this writing, I can already see how much I've changed. There were many, many people in my life who helped me walk through the deep sadness that I expressed through much of this writing. Though none walked as closely nor as consistently as my two closest friends, Kate and Lu, and my boyfriend Thomas.

After some time passes after someone dies, it can feel like everyone forgot about it. I found myself often wanting to say "Hey, do you remember? Do you know what happened in my life a couple of months ago?' But these three, they never forgot. And of course, nobody forgets, but it simply isn't a big part of their lives anymore. It was a big thing to them the week that it happened, the day of his wake and his funeral. But then life begins again. Something annoying happens at work, you realize you forgot to take out the chicken to thaw for dinner, or you miss a flight. Life gets annoying again, and the clarity that devastation brings is muddled.

I was so incredibly lucky that while these three people's lives got muddy again, they never moved on from my clarity. They each loved me in distinct and beautiful ways. Thomas still sends me a picture of the sunset every night and talks to me about my dad often. Lu makes fun of me in the same way that my dad always did, and also consistently reminds me that he would want me to be truly happy. Kate, well Kate sat in the mess with me and never asked me to clean it up.

They each heard my blood-curdling screams and were not moved an inch.

As I finish this book, I am beginning the process of moving to Denver to pursue a Master's in Clinical Mental Health and School Counseling. I am moving towards being able to speak of my dad with a sense of nostalgia, rather than solely one of deep sadness (an idea I discovered from one of my favorite follows on the internet, Gretchen Geraghty, who also lost her dad when she was twenty-two). I can truly laugh without feeling a weight on my chest. I, for the first time in so long, feel like I can live.

This does not mean that I have moved on. My dad, his life, his cancer trek, and his memory, is not something that I will ever move on from. Instead, I am attempting to do as one of my favorite authors Nora McInerny instructs us to do in the wake of grief and "move forward".

In her Ted Talk, *We Don't "Move On" from Grief. We Move Forward With It*, Nora talks about losing her husband Aaron to the same disease my dad died of, Glioblastoma. At that same time, she had a miscarriage with their second baby and also lost her dad. Nora, like so many people, deeply understands grief because she has deeply loved. She loved Aaron in the same way that I watched parents love each other, with everything they had. She was widowed young, and as a part of her work, she started a group called the "Hot Young Widows Club" with another friend of hers that was also a young widow.

She asked this group about some of the unhelpful things people said to them during their grief. She found that one thing stood out, how they needed to move on. McInerny talks about how much she hated that phrase, and why she understood why others did, too. Because to her, and to me, moving on means that "Aaron's life and death and love are just moments [she] can leave behind me". She talks about how this just doesn't speak to her experience because her husband is still so present to her.

She makes the distinction that it is not in the "churchy way people tried to tell [her] that he would be". Instead, Aaron still is. "He is just indelible, and still so present for [her]". That is exactly how I feel about my dad. He is still so present because he still is. I wonder if that is what happens when you love well, that you just stick around in an indescribable way.

Zach has grown up so much and he is starting to look more and more like my dad. I look at him, and I know my dad still is. I listen to Ron make plans for his future, and I know my dad still is. I talk to Mr. Jim, and I feel like I am talking to my dad because my dad still is.

I would trade all of this knowledge and the dog we got (sorry Boots), to have him back. I would trade the empathy, the understanding, and the deep character growth I have gone through. But in the absence of that, these things I will take. With my Father in Heaven and my dad in Heaven with him, I will choose to be kinder, more loving, and braver until I see them both face to face. When I hear the blood-curdling cries of others, whether they be those of my future children or those in deep grief, I will not be moved. I will take all of the love that was extended to my family during this time, and I will give it away.

I will choose to take this Sacred Year, and let it lead to a good life.

Works Referenced

Brown, Brené. *Atlas of the Heart: Mapping Meaningful Connection and the Language of Human Experience*. Random House Large Print, 2022.

Lewis, C.S. "A Grief Observed". Faber and Faber, 1973.

Lewis, C.S. *The Magician's Nephew*. Collins, 1980.

McInerny, Nora. "We Don't "Move On" from Grief. We Move Forward With It." *TED*, 2018, https://www.ted.com/talks/nora_mcinerny_we_don_t_move_on_from_grief_we_move_forward_with_it.

Niequist, Shauna. *Present over Perfect: Leaving Behind Frantic For a Simpler, More Soulful Way of Living*. Center Point Large Print, 2017.

Secondhand Lions directed by Tim McCanlies, performances by Micheal Caine, Robert Duvall, and Haley Joel Osment, New Line Cinema, 2003.